# THE SCOPES TRIAL

## The Battle Over Teaching Evolution

by Stephanie Fitzgerald

◆

SNAPSHOTS

# THE SCOPES TRIAL

## The Battle Over Teaching Evolution

By Stephanie Fitzgerald

Content Adviser: Margaret Barnett, Ph.D., Professor of History,
University of Southern Mississippi

Reading Adviser: Katie Van Sluys, Ph.D.,
School of Education, DePaul University

Compass Point Books ✦ Minneapolis, Minnesota

## ✦ Compass Point Books

3109 West 50th Street, #115
Minneapolis, MN 55410

Visit Compass Point Books on the Internet at
*www.compasspointbooks.com*
or e-mail your request to
*custserv@compasspointbooks.com*

For Compass Point Books
Jennifer VanVoorst, Jaime Martens, XNR Productions, Inc.,
Catherine Neitge, Keith Griffin, and Carol Jones

Produced by White-Thomson Publishing Ltd.

For White-Thomson Publishing
Stephen White-Thomson, Susan Crean, Amy Sparks,
Tinstar Design Ltd., Margaret Barnett, Peggy Bresnick Kendler,
Will Hare, and Timothy Griffin

**Library of Congress Cataloging-in-Publication Data**
Fitzgerald, Stephanie.
  The Scopes trial : the battle over teaching evolution / By Stephanie
Fitzgerald.
      p. cm. — (Snapshots in history)
  Includes bibliographical references and index.
  ISBN-13: 978-0-7565-2018-2 (library binding)
  ISBN-10: 0-7565-2018-5 (library binding)
  ISBN-13: 978-0-7565-2019-9 (paperback)
  ISBN-10: 0-7565-2019-3 (paperback)
1.  Scopes, John Thomas—Trials, litigation, etc.—Juvenile literature. 2.
Evolution—Study and teaching—Law and legislation—Tennessee—
Juvenile literature. 3.  Scopes, John Thomas—Trials, litigation, etc.
4.  Evolution—Study and teaching—Law and legislation.  I. Title. II.
Series.
  KF224.S3F58 2006
  345.73'0288—dc22                                    2006027082

# CONTENTS

The Great Monkey Trial .............................8

Exploring Our Beginnings ........................16

Evolution in Schools................................28

A Storm Brews in Dayton ........................34

Court Is in Session...................................48

Classroom or Courtroom? ........................56

The Great Showdown ..............................66

Slow Progress..........................................78

Timeline..................................................86

On the Web.............................................89

Glossary..................................................90

Source Notes...........................................91

Select Bibliography/Further Reading ......93

Index ......................................................94

About the Author/Image Credits ............96

# The Great Monkey Trial

By 9 A.M. on July 10, 1925, the temperature in Dayton, Tennessee, was already unbearably high. All 700 seats were filled in the tiny Rhea County Courthouse. An additional 300 spectators lined the walls of the courtroom, sweating in the Southern heat. People tried to keep cool by waving fans made from palm fronds or paper.

More than 200 newspaper reporters from all over the world had come to Dayton to witness a historic event. Twenty-two telegraph operators waited with their fingers on the telegraph keys, ready to report each day's developments. And for the first time in history, a trial would be broadcast over the radio. For the next week and a half, the eyes of the world would be focused on Dayton, where Trial Case No. 5232, *State of Tennessee v. John Thomas Scopes*, was being held.

*The courtroom in the Rhea County Courthouse in Dayton, Tennessee, was home to one of the most spectacular trials of the 20th century.*

In 1925, Dayton, Tennessee, was a quiet rural town with a population of just 1,800 people. There were only about 200 African-Americans living there—and no Catholic or Jewish people. The residents of Dayton were mostly fundamentalist Protestants, people who firmly believed that everything written in the Bible should be taken literally.

In the weeks prior to the Scopes trial, people from all over the country began pouring into Dayton. Before long, the town's one hotel was booked solid. Some visitors rented rooms in people's houses, while others slept in tents or under their cars.

Ordinarily, not many people would care about a trial concerning a schoolteacher in a small town. But this case was different. John Scopes, a science teacher and football coach at Dayton High School, was being tried for teaching evolution in school, a practice that had been outlawed in Tennessee earlier that year.

Many people thought—incorrectly—that the theory of evolution claimed that human beings were descended from monkeys. For this reason, the newspapers dubbed the Scopes trial the Monkey Trial.

In the days leading up to the trial, Dayton's sleepy main street took on a circuslike atmosphere. Peddlers selling Bibles, stuffed monkeys, and pins that read "Your Old Man's a Monkey" lined the streets. There were even circus performers with live chimpanzees there to entertain the children. Preachers set up tents all over the town, where they gave sermons. The citizens of Dayton welcomed all these visitors with open arms. Main Street and all its storefronts were decorated, people sold hotdogs and lemonade on the street, and the local drugstore offered a special new drink called monkey fizz.

*Visitors to Dayton seized upon the idea of a "monkey" trial.*

11

By 1925, the theory of evolution had become the accepted scientific explanation of how life on Earth gradually developed over time. It was a theory proposed about 65 years earlier by Charles Darwin. He had theorized that all life on Earth—including humans—had developed from primitive organisms. This was a shocking claim for people of the 19th century to accept.

Before the theory of evolution, many people in Europe and the United States believed that the story of creation as outlined in the Bible explained how life—and Earth itself—came into being. They believed that God created the first humans, Adam and Eve, who then began to populate Earth.

But as early as 1900, Darwin's theory had been backed up by scientists in other fields of study. And even most religious leaders accepted Darwin's findings. Still, there were some people who refused to question what was written in the Bible. These people, called fundamentalists, had broken from the mainline Protestant churches and many dedicated themselves to the fight against the acceptance and teaching of evolution.

In theory, John Scopes' attorneys were in Dayton to prove his innocence, and the prosecution team was there to prove his guilt. But that was not the real battle that would be fought in the Rhea County Courthouse. Scopes was charged with teaching the theory of evolution, something he openly admitted to doing.

The real battle being fought in Dayton was one between the theories of evolution and creationism. And the stars of the trial were not the citizens, the witnesses, or even the defendant. They were

*Teacher John Scopes had no idea how much attention his trial would come to attract.*

13

William Jennings Bryan and Clarence Darrow, two of the best-known speakers and attorneys in the United States. Both men had come from other parts of the country to take part in this fight.

Bryan was there to fight for creationism—to help the "good" of his beliefs triumph over the "evil" of evolution. He also wanted to make sure the Bible was upheld as the one true source of knowledge and learning.

Darrow was there to fight for progress, science, and academic freedom—as well as to discredit

*One thousand spectators filled the courtroom during the trial of John Scopes to witness the battle between evolution and creationism.*

what he considered "fool ideas that no intelligent Christian on earth believes."

This struggle was about something much larger than the guilt or innocence of one schoolteacher. And it would end with one of the greatest clashes on the witness stand in history. The trial would help shape curricula in American schools for years to come and help better define the freedoms afforded all Americans in the Bill of Rights. ◣

# Exploring Our Beginnings

## Chapter

2

For thousands of years, humans turned to stories from their religion to explain the world around them. Assuming that a god was in control of all life on Earth—from creating Earth and all its inhabitants to causing crops to grow or falter—was how people made sense of what they saw every day. For Christians, the answers to all of the questions about the natural world could be found in the Bible.

About 500 years ago, though, things began to change. A scientific revolution was taking place all over the world. At that time, the new field of science was transforming the way people thought about the world. Scientists started looking at the world in different ways and were no longer willing to accept what had always been believed. They looked for answers to many of their questions about the natural world through experimentation and close observation. However, the answers they discovered often contradicted what was written in the Bible.

Still, up until the 19th century, many Christians accepted what was written in the Bible's Book of Genesis as the literal story of creation: that about 6,000 years ago, God created Earth, the sun, and the moon; all the creatures in the sky, in the seas, and on the land; and the first humans, Adam and Eve, over the course of six days.

*A woodcut from 1530 depicts the story of creation.*

## EARLY CONFLICTS

In 1543, Nicolaus Copernicus, a Polish astronomer, published a book that proved Earth moved around the sun. Before then, people believed Earth was the center of the universe. Since his writings seemed to contradict the Bible, religious leaders decided that his findings were dangerous to religion. They tried to keep his views from spreading by any means possible—even killing men who taught Copernicus' theories. The most famous case of this censorship occurred when the Italian astronomer Galileo was imprisoned for believing in, and teaching, Copernicus' theories.

In the 1800s, as people learned more about Earth and how things worked, they began to see the Bible's story of creation as an allegory rather than as the literal truth. As scientists gained a greater understanding of the mysteries of how life really began on Earth, this theory of evolution became the accepted truth—but not for everyone.

Many discoveries were made, in all different scientific fields, which disproved creation as outlined in the Bible. When archaeologists uncovered fossilized plants and animals, they realized that a wide variety of different creatures had lived on Earth in the past.

The unearthing of these fossils also revealed that the rock that forms Earth is made of layers, which are stacked from oldest to newest. Each layer of rock contained different kinds of fossils. These pieces of information taken together showed that Earth had formed gradually over time, not in one day as claimed in the Bible. This evidence also showed that the creatures that lived on Earth had changed over time—they had not all been created at once and in their present form.

The rift between science and religion was completely blown open when Charles Darwin, a British naturalist, published his theory of evolution in 1859. Darwin's theory maintained that through a process called evolution, all living things change gradually over millions of years. During this time, certain species die out and other new species emerge.

*When he published* The Origin of Species, *Charles Darwin sparked a debate that would last for decades.*

19

The seeds for this theory were planted when Darwin was only 22 years old. On December 27, 1831, the young man signed on as an unpaid naturalist aboard the *H.M.S. Beagle*. The ship was embarking on a five-year voyage around the world.

For three years, Darwin sailed the open seas and visited the many islands where the *Beagle* docked. He often lived ashore for weeks at a time while he studied and collected the islands' plants and animals. The island visit that changed Darwin's life occurred in September 1835, when the *Beagle* approached the Galapagos Islands, a group of more than 15 islands that lies in the Pacific Ocean near Ecuador.

Up until then, the islands' only inhabitants had been animals, including gigantic tortoises, iguanas, and birds. For four weeks, Darwin hopped from island to island, cataloging the animals he found there. In observing the islands' finches, he made a discovery that would change the course of scientific study.

Darwin noticed that although finches lived on many of the islands, the birds were different from one island to the next. Each group of finches was slightly modified to best suit the needs of its survival on a particular island. For example, on an island where the birds ate seeds, the finches had large, powerful beaks suitable for breaking open their food. On islands where the birds ate insects, their beaks were smaller. For 20 years, the

naturalist thought about the various finches on the Galapagos Islands and constructed a theory of how animals evolve.

In 1859, Darwin published his findings in a book called *On the Origin of Species by Means of Natural Selection, or the Preservation of Favoured Races in the*

*The H.M.S Beagle sailed from England in 1831 to explore sites around the globe.*

21

*Darwin's observations of finches on the Galapagos Islands eventually led to his theory of evolution.*

*Struggle for Life*. It is more commonly known as *The Origin of Species*.

Darwin believed that evolution occurred through a process called natural selection. In general, this theory pointed out that most animals produce more offspring than their environment can support. This is balanced by the fact that many of the offspring never make it to adulthood—they are either killed by predators, lack of food, or changes in their environment.

He also pointed out that no two members of any plant or animal species are exactly alike. Every organism has a different combination of traits. Darwin believed that some members of each generation had the traits that made them better able to survive than others.

He reasoned that since those individuals are more likely to survive, they would pass on those traits to their offspring, who would likewise find it easier to survive. Those members of the species that did not have these particular traits were more likely to die out, ending their line of descent.

Darwin called this process "survival of the fittest." Over millions of years, the process resulted in the natural selection of species that survived and the extinction of other species.

Darwin went on to state that all life on Earth had started with a one-cell organism, which over billions of years evolved into many different types of more complex organisms. That meant that every plant and animal on Earth is descended from an earlier form of life.

As soon as Darwin's theories were made public, debate began to rage in his homeland. Some

Although Darwin's name is associated with the theory of evolution, he was not the first person to come up with the idea. A Greek scholar named Empedocles first suggested the idea of survival of the fittest more than 2,500 years ago. And in the 1800s, a French noble, the Chevalier de Lamarck, theorized that changes in an animal's environment could cause it to adapt until a new form of the animal appeared that was better suited to that environment. Though these men were exploring the notion of how organisms adapt and develop over time, they did not come to the conclusions that Darwin would. They were also just dealing with guesswork and did not have any evidence to support their ideas.

scientists took Darwin's side from the start, but most other people, including many religious leaders, argued against him. But even as both sides in Great Britain were arguing the point, the evidence to back up Darwin's theories was beginning to pile up.

In 1856, scientists discovered the fossilized skeletons of people who today are known as Neanderthals, which offered proof that there had been a primitive form of humans. Then the fossilized remains of a prehistoric creature called an Archaeopteryx, which was a combination of a bird and a reptile, were found. This proved Darwin's claim that birds had evolved from reptiles. Very quickly, most British scientists started to agree that Darwin's theory was correct.

In the meantime, the work of Gregor Mendel, an Austrian monk and botanist, proved Darwin's claim that genetic traits were handed down from generation to generation. Mendel had spent years crossbreeding thousands of pea plants and studying how certain traits developed in each generation of the plants.

*The half-reptile and half-bird Archaeopteryx fossil has been called a fossil caught in the act of evolution.*

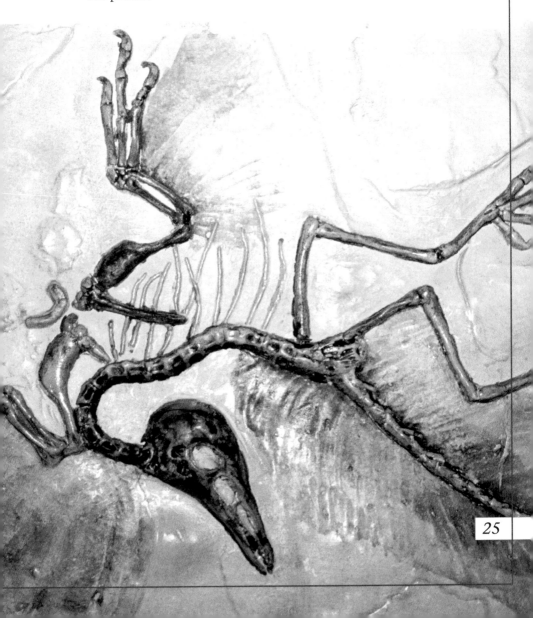

25

As a result of some of these findings and other scientific research and discoveries, virtually every scientist in the world accepted Darwin's theory of evolution as fact by the beginning of the 20th century.

Even many Christian leaders accepted evolution as fact. By 1900, the leaders of many Protestant churches had adjusted their teachings. They no longer required members to believe that the world and everything in it had literally been created in six days and that all the plants and animals had been created in exactly the same form as they exist

The Origin of Species *explored how plants and animals evolve over long periods of time.*

ON

# THE ORIGIN OF SPECIES

## BY MEANS OF NATURAL SELECTION,

OR THE

PRESERVATION OF FAVOURED RACES IN THE STRUGGLE FOR LIFE.

" But with regard to the material world, we can at least go so far as this—we can perceive that events are brought about not by insulated interpositions of Divine power, exerted in each particular case, but by the establishment of general laws."

W. WHEWELL: *Bridgewater Treatise.*

"To conclude, therefore, let no man out of a weak conceit of sobriety, or an ill-applied moderation, think or maintain, that a man can search too far or be too well studied in the book of God's word, or in the book of God's works; divinity or philosophy; but rather let men endeavour an endless progress or proficience in both."

BACON: *Advancement of Learning.*

By CHARLES DARWIN, M.A.,

FELLOW OF THE ROYAL, GEOLOGICAL, LINNÆAN, ETC., SOCIETIES; AUTHOR OF 'JOURNAL OF RESEARCHES DURING H. M. S. BEAGLE'S VOYAGE ROUND THE WORLD.'

Linnean Society of London.

*Down, Bromley, Kent, October 1st, 1859.*

LONDON: JOHN MURRAY, ALBEMARLE STREET. 1859.

*The right of Translation is reserved.*

today. Nor were members required to believe that the first humans, Adam and Eve, were created by God to be the originators of the human race.

This new way of thinking led the fundamentalist Protestants to split from their churches in the early 1900s. The fundamentalists contended that people could either believe in the Bible or in Darwin's theory of evolution, but that the two ideas could not coexist. In fact, they considered a belief in evolution to be sinful. Opposing the teaching of the theory of evolution became a defining cause of the fundamentalist movement that still exists today. ◥

## WHAT'S IN A NAME?

Fundamentalists took their name from a group of 12 religious pamphlets called *The Fundamentals*, which were written and published from 1910 to 1915. These books listed the five essential truths that all Christians should believe:

- Everything written in the Bible is absolutely true.
- All of the miracles described in the Bible were authentic.
- Mary was a virgin when she gave birth to Jesus Christ.
- Christ voluntarily died to atone for the sins of humanity.
- Christ was resurrected.

# Evolution in Schools

By the turn of the century, evolution was being taught in most biology courses around the United States. This made fundamentalists nervous—they worried that learning about evolution would turn their children away from religion. As a result, fundamentalists worked hard to keep evolution out of the classrooms. They made the most headway in the area of the United States known as the Bible Belt. This area covered most of the Southern United States and stretched west across Texas and as far north as Kansas and parts of Virginia.

In 1922, a bill forbidding the teaching of the theory of evolution made it all the way to a final vote in the Kentucky state legislature. It was defeated by a tiny margin: 42 votes to 41.

*By the early 1900s, evolution was taught in most U.S. classrooms.*

## The Bible Belt

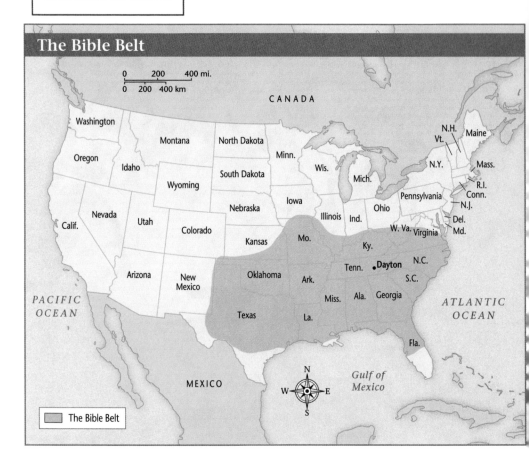

*The Bible Belt*

*The Southeastern part of the United States is known as the Bible Belt.*

The next year, a similar bill was introduced in Florida. That bill was defeated, too, although the legislature did pass a resolution urging teachers not to teach evolution.

The fundamentalists enjoyed a small victory in Oklahoma, where a bill was passed that said textbooks could not include statements about evolution. But that did not really stop the teaching of evolution. In North Carolina, an anti-evolution bill was defeated in 1924, but all biology textbooks that covered evolution were removed from the state's high schools.

Although they had not had much success in getting anti-evolution legislation passed, the fundamentalists continued their crusade. On March 13, 1925, they scored their first major victory when the Butler Act was signed into law in Tennessee.

The Butler Act, which was named after John Washington Butler, the Tennessee legislator who proposed it, read in part:

*[It] shall be unlawful for any teacher in any of the Universities ... and all other public schools of the State which are supported in whole or in part by the public school funds of the State, to teach any theory that denies the story of the Divine Creation of man as taught in the Bible, and to teach instead that man has descended from a lower order of animals. ...*

*That any teacher found guilty of the violation of this Act, shall be guilty of a misdemeanor and upon conviction, shall be fined not less than One Hundred ($100.00) Dollars nor more than Five Hundred ($500.00) Dollars for each offense.*

This law was passed despite the fact that, for the most part, the people who voted on it did not feel very strongly about the issue. The members

## A STIFF PENALTY

The fine for violating the Butler Law might not sound like a lot today. But in 1925, $100 was a lot of money—especially for schoolteachers, whose average yearly salary was only around $800.

31

of the Tennessee House of Representatives and the Senate had to answer to the people who elected them. Those people were mainly fundamentalists. These politicians knew that if they voted against the Butler Act, the people they represented would not vote for them again.

The Tennessee House of Representatives approved the bill by a vote of 71-5. Those who voted for it probably expected the members of the Tennessee Senate to kill it. But when the bill got to the Senate, it was passed by a vote of 24-6. Most of the members of the Senate expected Tennessee Governor Austin Peay to veto the bill.

But Governor Peay had his own reasons for signing the bill into law. He was planning to run for the U.S. Senate and he needed the support of the people in his state. Still, his motives were not completely selfish. The governor was also trying to get more money for the schools. That would mean asking the representatives of relatively poor people—most of whom were fundamentalists—to support a tax increase. He did not feel that he could veto the Butler Act and then get support for a tax increase for education.

Governor Peay further justified signing the bill into law by stating:

*After careful examination I can find nothing of consequence in the books now being taught in our schools with which this bill will interfere in the slightest manner. Therefore, it will not put our teachers in any jeopardy.*

*Tennessee Governor Austin Peay signed the Butler Act into law.*

Of course, there was no way Peay could know then that this very bill would lead to one of the most important court battles of the 20th century.

# A Storm Brews in Dayton

*Chapter*

*4*

The Butler Law became the first law on the books prohibiting the teaching of evolution in Tennessee schools. But that would not be the end of the story.

No law passed in the United States, whether it is made on a local, state, or federal level, can contradict what is written in the U.S. Constitution. Likewise, no state or local law can contradict what is written in a state's constitution, which itself is based largely on the U.S. Constitution.

When the Butler Law was passed, some people around the country thought it went against what was written in the U.S. Constitution. The way to determine the constitutionality of a law is to bring a test case, or a case set up simply to challenge the constitutionality of the law, to court. However, local, city, and county courts cannot decide whether a law is constitutional. Only a state supreme court or the U.S. Supreme Court can make that decision.

*Some people wanted to challenge the Butler Law in the U.S. Supreme Court.*

Lucille Milner was the secretary of the American Civil Liberties Union (ACLU) when the Butler Law was passed. One of her jobs was to look through the nation's newspapers and cut out any articles of interest to the organization. Examples of these would be news articles about court cases in which a defendant might need the help of an ACLU lawyer or reports about laws that had

## THE ACLU

The American Civil Liberties Union (ACLU), established in 1920, has had the same goals for more than 80 years. The ACLU works to defend the U.S. Constitution—especially the Bill of Rights—by fighting against unfair or unjust laws. The organization provides free legal aid to any person who is prosecuted under such laws, especially those unable to afford a lawyer.

been passed that violated civil rights. When she came across an item about the passage of the Butler Law in a Tennessee newspaper, Milner knew right away that it would be of interest to the ACLU.

When Milner showed the newspaper story to members of the board of directors of the ACLU, they quickly determined that the Butler Law was unconstitutional. They believed that making it illegal to teach evolution was interfering with a teacher's right to free speech—a right that is guaranteed in the First Amendment to the Constitution. They also felt that the religious element of the law opposed the idea of the separation of church and state, which is also spelled out in the First Amendment.

The members of the ACLU decided to put together a test case to challenge the constitutionality of the law. First they would have to find someone to break the law. Then they would bring that person's case to a county court, where they would most likely lose.

Once their client, the defendant, was found guilty, ACLU attorneys would appeal the verdict by bringing their case to a higher court—the state supreme court. This would give them the opportunity to challenge the constitutionality of the law. If, during that proceeding, the attorneys could prove that the law was unconstitutional, the court would abolish, or strike down, the law. A state supreme court can abolish a state law, but only the U.S. Supreme Court can strike down a federal law.

The ACLU sent a press release to all the Tennessee newspapers asking for a volunteer for their test case. The press release stated that if any teacher would agree to be arrested for violating the new law, the ACLU would provide the best attorneys in the country and would take care of the teacher's financial needs.

On the morning of May 5, 1925, a group of men were gathered in Robinson's Drugstore in downtown Dayton, Tennessee. They included the owner of the drugstore, F. E. "Doc" Robinson, who was also the chairman of the Rhea County School Board, Walter White, the Rhea County school superintendent, attorneys Wallace Haggard and brothers Herbert and Sue Hicks, and a mining engineer named George Rappelyea.

Rappelyea mentioned to the other men that he had read about the ACLU's offer. He said it would be a good idea if they could test the law in Dayton. He knew that holding a trial there would bring a lot of attention—and a lot of business—to their little town.

The rest of the men liked Rappelyea's idea, but they wondered which teacher they could get to stand trial. It would have made the most sense to put the high school biology teacher on trial. After all, he was the most likely person to have taught

*Downtown Dayton, Tennessee, was home to Robinson's Drugstore, where the men who planned the Scopes test case often met.*

evolution. But the school's biology teacher, William Ferguson, was married with children. The group did not think it would be right to ask him to get arrested and stand trial.

Then one of the men mentioned John Scopes, a science teacher and the football coach at Dayton High. Although he had not taught biology regularly, he had substituted for Ferguson, helping the students prepare for final exams. Scopes was 24 years old, single, and very well liked. He seemed like the perfect candidate.

Rappelyea sent a boy from the drugstore down to the high school, where Scopes was playing tennis with a student. He was instructed to bring the teacher back to the drugstore right away. When Scopes arrived at Robinson's, still in his sweaty tennis gear, the men gathered there told him about their plan.

They asked the young teacher whether he thought it was possible to teach biology without teaching about evolution. Scopes replied that it was not. Then he took down a copy of *Civic Biology*, which was sold along with other textbooks at Robinson's. He showed the men that this book, which had been the official biology book for Tennessee schools since 1919, contained an overview of Darwin's theories. Everyone had a good laugh about the fact that the Butler Law did not take into consideration that the teaching of evolution in Tennessee schools had already been approved for many years.

Scopes could not remember teaching his students about evolution. But the men determined that since Scopes had reviewed the whole term's work, for the students, he must have broken the Butler Law by covering evolution as well. Then Doc Robinson asked Scopes whether he would be willing to be part of the ACLU's test case.

Scopes agreed at once. Since the ACLU would pay all of his legal fees as well as any fines in case he was found guilty, Scopes really had nothing to lose. There was more to his participation than that, though. As he later wrote in his memoirs:

> *I had been taught from childhood to stand up for what I thought was right and I did not think the state of Tennessee had any right to keep me from teaching the truth. So I was willing to test the law's constitutionality. If*

*Scopes (seated, second from left) showed the organizers of the test case that evolution was included in a Tennessee school book.*

> *the result has served freedom, then I must give much of the credit to my own parents and to a tolerant environment that taught me early in life to revere truth and love and courage.*

Scopes returned to his tennis game while the rest of the men worked out the details of their plan. They decided that attorneys Sue and Herbert Hicks and Wallace Haggard could be the prosecuting attorneys in the case and that John Godsey, a former judge who since retiring had been working in a private law practice, could defend the teacher.

Then Rappelyea sent a telegram to the ACLU offices in New York with the news that he had a candidate for a test case. The ACLU quickly responded with an offer of the promised help, plus publicity. That same day, May 5, 1925, John Scopes was officially charged with violating the Butler Law and was arrested, though he was not jailed.

Before anyone can be put on trial in some cases, he or she has to be indicted, or formally accused of breaking the law, by a grand jury. During a preliminary hearing, a pretrial jury hears the facts of the case and decides whether there is enough evidence to bring the defendant to trial. The grand jury in the *Scopes* case met on May 25 and quickly indicted the teacher.

As soon as the news got out that a test case of the Tennessee anti-evolution law was being tried in Dayton, the small-town attorneys began receiving offers of help from around the country.

One of the earliest volunteers offered his services to Scopes' defense team. John R. Neal, who was the head of a law school in Knoxville, Tennessee, was friendly with Godsey. After the two men spoke about the case, Neal offered to help. Although he did not have a strong opinion on evolution, Neal was one of the top attorneys when it came to matters involving the Constitution. Just as important, he felt very strongly that Tennessee's anti-evolution law violated academic freedom—a teacher's right to teach about any legitimate subject and a school's right to determine what it would teach.

Neal was well known locally, but few people outside Tennessee had ever heard of him. The next volunteer, this time for the prosecution, had a much higher profile. The name William Jennings Bryan was known by just about every adult citizen of the United States.

Bryan had represented Nebraska in Congress and had run for president as the Democratic candidate three times—in 1896, 1900, and 1908. Although Bryan never won, he did achieve great standing in the Democratic Party and helped shape its policies. He also served as U.S. secretary of state from 1913 to 1915 under President Woodrow Wilson.

Bryan had very liberal views for his time. He supported a woman's right to vote in federal elections—a right that was not granted until 1920—as well as a federal income tax and the establishment of the Department of Labor. He also

## GRAND GESTURE

William Jennings Bryan resigned from his post as secretary of state on June 9, 1915. He had counseled President Woodrow Wilson against actions that he knew would lead the United States into World War I. When Wilson repeatedly ignored Bryan's advice, Bryan gave up the only national office he ever held. Bryan felt he had to do his duty according to his conscience, even though the move would halt his political career.

stood up for working people and farmers, a trait that earned him the nickname the "Great Commoner." To his enemies, though, Bryan was known as the "Great Windbag."

Bryan was a deeply religious man who did not approve of the teaching of evolution. He believed the story of creation as told in the Bible and felt the teaching of evolution would turn children away from religion. In fact, he felt that the theory of evolution was actually dangerous—and was a big cause of World War I. He believed that the idea of the survival of the fittest was what had led Germany to go to war. In the early 1900s, fighting against the teaching of evolution became the focus of Bryan's considerable influence.

After retiring from politics, Bryan concentrated on preaching. He had always been an amazing speechmaker. Now, rather than preaching about government reform, he preached about the Bible and its teachings.

*William Jennings Bryan had liberal views for his time, but he was also a deeply religious man.*

Bryan traveled around the country sharing his views on evolution. In a speech that he delivered often, called "The Menace of Darwinism," Bryan made his position clear. He said, in part:

> *It is better to trust in the Rock of Ages than to know the ages of rocks; it is better for one to know that he is close to the Heavenly Father than to know how far the stars in the heavens are apart.*

Bryan played an active role in the fundamentalist effort to get anti-evolution laws passed in the South. He knew many politicians in the state legislatures from his time in government and persuaded them to introduce anti-evolution bills. Then he worked to persuade legislators to pass those bills.

In May 1925, when Bryan heard about the Scopes trial, he stated that he would like to volunteer his services to the prosecution. This offer, which was printed in the newspaper, was read by the Hicks brothers. They quickly wrote to Bryan, telling him how honored they would be if he joined their team. He agreed.

Bryan's joining the prosecution was front-page news around the nation. And it quickly led to more offers of help for the defense team, too. One of the attorneys who volunteered his services was as well known as Bryan. His name was Clarence Darrow, and he was the most famous trial attorney in the United States.

Darrow gained fame after quitting a high-paying job with a railroad company to defend the head of the American Railway Union, Eugene V. Debs, in 1895. Debs, who was leading a strike against the railroad, had been portrayed as a violent, dangerous man who was trying to stir up trouble against the government.

Many people wondered why Darrow would defend such a person. But Darrow demonstrated in court that Debs was fighting to improve the working conditions of railroad workers, who worked in horrible circumstances for very little pay. He also pointed out how the railroad had broken laws in order to frame Debs.

The trial showed the world that Darrow was a brilliant attorney who cared about the problems of the common person. He quickly gained a reputation for defending the poorest and most downtrodden people.

45

Interestingly, Darrow stood for many of the same liberal beliefs that Bryan did. In fact, he had even supported Bryan the first time Bryan ran for president. There was one major difference between the two men, however: Bryan was a fundamentalist and Darrow was an agnostic—someone who believes it is impossible to know whether God exists.

Darrow felt very strongly that the fundamentalists posed a serious threat to religious and academic freedom in the United States. The Scopes trial offered him the chance to fight the fundamentalists, represented by Bryan, face to face in a national forum. As he later recalled:

*For the first, the last, the only time in my life, I volunteered my services in a case ... because I really wanted to take part in it. ... From any point of view, the law [Butler Law] was silly and senseless. ... I was in New York not long after the arrest of Mr. Scopes, and saw that Mr. Bryan had volunteered to go to Dayton to assist in the prosecution. At once I wanted to go. My object, and my only object, was to focus the attention of the country on the programme of Mr. Bryan and the other fundamentalists in America. I knew that education was in danger from the source that has always hampered it—religious fanaticism.*

When Darrow volunteered for the defense, he brought another successful attorney with him, Dudley Field Malone. Malone, like Bryan, had been very active in the Democratic Party. In fact, he served as assistant secretary of state under Bryan in 1913.

Although he did not have a stated opinion on the theory of evolution, Malone was a firm believer in academic freedom and freedom of speech. He felt that anti-evolution laws sought to destroy these freedoms. Darrow later described Malone this way:

> *More than most men that one meets, Mr. Malone believes in freedom, in the right of every one to investigate for himself, and he resented the interference of the State in its effort to forbid or control the convictions and mental attitudes of men.*

More attorneys were also added to each team's roster. Arthur Garfield Hays, who was an ACLU attorney, joined the defense, as did F.B. McElwee, John R. Neal's law partner. As more attorneys volunteered for service, Scopes' original attorney, John Godsey, decided to drop out.

The final prosecution team was made up of the two Hicks brothers, Wallace Haggard, Ben G. McKenzie, and J. Gordon McKenzie, all Dayton attorneys, plus Bryan and his son, William Jennings Bryan Jr. A. Thomas Stewart, the attorney general for the 18th Judicial Circuit of Tennessee, led the prosecution team. Judge John Raulston of Dayton would be presiding over the trial.

## FUNDAMENTALIST FEAR

John Godsey, who was very religious, began to think that other fundamentalists would resent him for arguing against the anti-evolution law. After he left the defense team, Godsey apologized to the people of Dayton for being involved at all.

# Court Is in Session

Friday, July 10, 1925, marked the first day of the Scopes trial. Since the grand jury that had indicted Scopes in May had been rushed, it was decided that a new grand jury should be sworn in to decide on Scopes' indictment.

Attorney General Stewart read the same indictment that had been read in May to the grand jury. It stated in part that:

> *[Scopes] did unlawfully and willfully teach in public schools of Rhea County, Tennessee … certain theory and theories that deny the story of Divine creation of man as taught in the Bible and did teach thereof that man descended from a lower order of animals.*

Then Judge Raulston picked up the Bible and read the entire first chapter of Genesis to the jury so they could hear what the Christian version of creation was. The grand jury retired briefly to discuss the matter before returning with the new indictment. At 11 A.M., the trial of *State of Tennessee v. John Thomas Scopes* was ready to begin.

The first item on the defense's agenda was a motion to quash the indictment. According to John R. Neal, the anti-evolution Butler Law violated the Tennessee Constitution on 13 counts.

*John Scopes (seated, right) had an expert defense team, which included Dudley Malone (center) and Arthur Garfield Hays (standing). Scopes' father, Thomas (left), was also on hand to lend moral support.*

Then Clarence Darrow stood up and introduced a topic that would turn into a familiar argument throughout the rest of the trial. He told the judge that the defense planned to call on expert witnesses in the fields of science and religion. These experts had traveled from around the country to be in Dayton, and Darrow wanted to let them know how long they would have to wait before being called to testify.

But Judge Raulston believed the most pressing concern of the trial was to select the jury. All other questions could wait. The rest of the day was spent selecting the 12 men who would decide on Scopes' guilt or innocence. At the time, women were not allowed to serve on a jury in Tennessee.

When the court met again on Monday morning, the defense once again moved to quash the indictment. No one denied that Scopes had broken the Butler Law. The more important issue to the defense was whether that law was unconstitutional. If the defense managed to quash the indictment that day, the only way the

### QUASHING AN INDICTMENT

To quash an indictment means to throw it out of court. Most defense attorneys will make this their first argument in a case. If the attorneys can come up with a sound legal reason why their client should not stand trial for the crime for which he or she has been accused, the entire case can be thrown out of court.

prosecution could keep the anti-evolution law on the books would be to appeal the case to the state Supreme Court.

Neal—a Tennessee Constitution expert—focused on Section 12, Article II of the Tennessee state constitution as part of his first argument. It said:

> *Knowledge, learning, and virtue, being essential to the preservation of republican institutions ... it shall be the duty of the general assembly in all future periods of this government, to cherish literature and science.*

According to Neal, the legislature could not possibly cherish science, nor could science be taught or studied, without including the theory of evolution. Therefore, he argued, the Butler Law violated the constitution. Next he read from the part of the state constitution concerning freedom of religion:

> *That all men have a natural and indefeasible right to worship Almighty God according to the dictates of their own conscience ... and that no preference shall ever be given by law, to any religious establishment or mode of worship.*

Obviously the Butler Law gave preference to Christianity, a fact that was easily overlooked in a town where everyone was Christian. The prosecution did not agree that this was a violation of the constitution, though. According to them, because the Bible was recognized throughout the country as a spiritual guide, the law was not really giving preference to one religion over another.

That afternoon, Darrow gave his first real speech of the trial when he presented a summary of the defense's case. He began by calling the Butler Law "as brazen and as bold an attempt to destroy learning as was ever made in the middle ages." He then continued:

*The Bible is not one book. The Bible is made up of sixty-six books written over a period of about one thousand years. ... It is a book primarily of religion and morals. It is not a book of science. ... The man who looked out at the universe and studied the heavens had no thought but that Earth was the center of the universe. But we know better than that. ... They thought Earth was created 4,004 years before the Christian Era. We know better. I doubt if there is a person in Tennessee who does not know better. They told it the best they knew.*

Darrow warned that the Butler Law could lead to religious bigotry and hatred among people of different beliefs. He also cautioned that a law prohibiting the teaching of evolution could lead to further censorship:

*If today you can take a thing like evolution and make it a crime to teach it in the public school, tomorrow you can make it a crime to teach it in the private schools, and the next year you can make it a crime to teach it ... in the church. At the next session you may ban books and the newspapers. Soon you may set*

*Catholic against Protestant and Protestant against Protestant, and try to foist your own religion upon the minds of men. If you can do one you can do the other. Ignorance and fanaticism is ever busy and needs feeding. Always it is feeding and gloating for more.*

On Wednesday, after two days of debate, Judge Raulston ruled against the defense's motion to quash the indictment. It was time for the defense to enter its plea of not guilty.

*Hundreds of spectators listened to the Scopes trial over loudspeakers set up outside the courthouse.*

The prosecution's opening statement was brief. Attorney General Stewart said:

> *John Thomas Scopes has violated ... what is known as the anti-evolution law, by teaching in the public schools of Rhea County the theory tending to show that man and mankind is descended from a lower order of animals. Therefore, he has taught a theory which denies the story of Divine Creation of man as taught by the Bible.*

Attorney Malone then spoke for the defense and explained his team's purpose. They intended, of course, to try to prove Scopes' innocence. But their broader goal was to show that the Bible was a religious book and had nothing to do with science. "We maintain that science and religion embrace

*Dudley Malone made the opening statement for the defense team. His speeches won admiration from trial spectators.*

two separate and distinct fields of thought and learning," he said. In other words, even though Scopes had taught evolution, his actions did not defy the Bible, since science and the Bible were not in competition with one another.

The prosecution was first to call its witnesses. First to take the stand was school superintendent Walter White, one of the men who had persuaded Scopes to stand trial. During questioning, White stated that at their meeting in Robinson's Drugstore, Scopes had admitted to teaching his students evolution.

Under cross-examination, Darrow got White to testify that the textbook Scopes had used, *Civic Biology*, was the state's official biology book. White further admitted that after the Butler Law was passed, neither he nor the school had warned teachers that they would be breaking the law by teaching from that textbook.

The prosecution then called two of Scopes' students to the witness stand. Both Harry Shelton and Howard Morgan testified individually that Scopes had taught them Darwin's theory about life evolving from lower organisms. When Darrow cross-examined the boys for the defense, he showed that Scopes' teachings did not cause either boy to leave the church or question his religion.

Finally, the prosecution called Doc Robinson to the stand. After he testified to hearing Scopes admitting to teaching evolution, the prosecution rested its case. 

55

# Classroom or Courtroom?

Once the prosecution rested on Wednesday afternoon, it was time for the defense to bring up the question of expert witnesses. The defense wanted these scientists and religious experts to offer testimony that clearly explained what the theory of evolution was and how it did not conflict with what was written in the Bible.

The prosecution, however, did not think that the expert testimony would be relevant to the case. The prosecuters accused the defense team of trying to turn the courtroom into a classroom. In the minds of the prosecution, the question was simply whether Scopes had broken the law by teaching evolution. They wanted the judge to rule against the defense and forbid the testimony from expert witnesses.

For the judge to decide on whether the expert witnesses would be allowed, he would need to hear the testimony of one witness, which would serve as a sample. But the judge did not think the members of the jury should hear the arguments about expert witnesses, in case he decided to rule against the defense. So the jury was asked to exit the courtroom.

The sample witness called by Darrow was Dr. Maynard M. Metcalf, a zoologist. He was also a dedicated member of the Congregational Church.

*The jury in the Scopes trial waited outside while the court decided whether to allow expert witnesses to give evidence.*

By choosing a man of science who was also deeply religious, Scopes' attorneys wanted to show that a person could believe in evolution without losing his or her faith.

During his testimony, Metcalf explained what scientists mean by the term "theory," as in the theory of evolution. When a scientist refers to something as a theory, it means a logical explanation for a set of established facts. It does not refer to a guess, as many nonscientists might think.

Darrow asked Metcalf about his experience in the field of zoology, as well as about his educational and religious background. Then he asked him whether he knew any scientists who did not believe in Darwin's theory of evolution. Metcalf responded:

> I am acquainted with practically all of the zoologists, botanists, and geologists of this country. ... I know there is not a single one among them who has the least doubt of the fact of evolution.

Court was adjourned on Wednesday afternoon before Metcalf finished giving his testimony, so Darrow planned to recall him to the stand on Thursday morning. Before he got the chance,

## THE WALLS HAVE EARS

The jury had been ordered out of the courtroom for the argument regarding expert witnesses. But that did not do much good. The jurors merely waited outside the courthouse, where loudspeakers had been set up so that spectators who did not make it inside could listen to the trial.

though, the prosecution team renewed its objections to expert testimony. Again, Darrow argued that it was important for the jury to have a clear understanding of evolution and that it was crucial to the case. He said, in part:

> *We expect to show by men of science and learning—both scientists and real scholars of the Bible … first what evolution is, and, secondly, that any interpretation of the Bible that intelligent men could possibly make*

*Dr. Maynard Metcalf was one of the experts the defense team wanted to place on the witness stand.*

Clarence Darrow
was a passionate
speaker and a
skilled attorney.

*is not in conflict with any story of creation, while the Bible, in many ways, is in conflict with every known science, and there isn't a human being on earth believes it literally. We expect to show that it isn't in conflict with the theory of evolution ... and we insist that a jury cannot decide this important question which means the final battle ground between science and religion ... without knowing both what evolution is and the interpretation of the story of creation.*

The attorneys argued back and forth for the rest of the morning while most of the spectators filed out of the courtroom. Listening to attorneys argue the fine points of law and procedure was not all that interesting. In fact, knowing that Bryan would speak again after lunch was probably the only thing that brought the crowd back to the courtroom that afternoon.

After lunch, the courtroom was filled to overflowing. All the fundamentalists in the area had been waiting to hear their hero speak. Although he was an older man, overweight, and wilting a bit in the summer heat, Bryan was still an impressive speaker. He explained that he had stayed out of the earlier arguments because there was something a lot more important at stake than legal technicalities. He explained to his listeners:

> *The people of this state knew what they were doing when they passed the law, and they knew the dangers of the doctrine [theory of evolution]—that they did not want it taught to their children. … Your Honor, it isn't proper to bring experts in here to try to defeat the purpose of the people of this state by trying to show that this thing that they denounce and outlaw is a beautiful thing that everybody ought to believe in. … The question is can a minority in this state come in and compel a teacher to teach that the Bible is not true and make the parents of these children pay the expenses of the teacher to tell their children what these people believe is false and dangerous?*

It was more a speech for a church than for a courtroom, and the crowd loved it. No sooner had Bryan stopped speaking than the courtroom rang with applause and cheers. People were out of their seats, surrounding Bryan and patting him on his back. As Darrow watched the reaction, he posed a pointed question to Arthur Garfield Hays, an attorney from the ACLU. "Can it be possible," Darrow asked, "that this trial is taking place in the 20th century?"

After a short recess, Dudley Malone rose to offer the defense's last argument of the day:

*Mr. Bryan quoted Mr. Darwin. That theory was evolved and explained by Mr. Darwin seventy-five years ago. Have we learned nothing in seventy-five years? ... Are we to hold mankind to a literal understanding of the claim that the world is 6,000 years old, because of the limited vision of men who believed the world was flat, and that Earth was the center of the universe, and that man is the center of Earth? ... Are we to have our children know nothing about science except what the church says they shall know? I have never seen harm in learning and understanding, in humility and open-mindedness, and I have never seen clearer the need of that learning than when I see the attitude of the prosecution, who attack and refuse to accept the information and intelligence, which expert witnesses will give them.*

*I feel that the prosecution here is filled with a needless fear. I believe that if they withdraw their objection and hear the evidence of our experts their minds would not only be improved but their souls would be purified.*

*For God's sake let the children have their minds kept open—close no doors to their knowledge; shut no door from them. Make the distinction between theology and science. Let them have both. Let them both be taught. Let them both live.*

*We are ready to tell the truth as we understand it and we do not fear all the truth that they can present as facts. We are ready. We are ready. We feel we stand with progress. We feel we stand with science. We feel we stand with intelligence. We feel we stand with fundamental freedom in America. We are not afraid.*

*Dudley Malone's speech completely overshadowed Bryan's speech.*

63

Incredibly, the crowd's response to Malone's speech was even more passionate than its response to Bryan's. The deafening applause lasted more than 15 minutes. When the crowd finally settled down again, Attorney General A. Thomas Stewart made a powerful speech of his own for the prosecution.

Stewart argued that if experts were allowed to testify about whether people's beliefs in the Bible were wrong, it would only be the start of many legal battles involving the Bible. He said that starting that controversy would not do anything to help the jury decide the *Scopes* case and, in fact, would only lead to more questions.

*Attorney General A. Thomas Stewart (standing) led the prosecution, though William Jennings Bryan is the most famous and best-remembered member of that team.*

At the end of the day, as the courtroom emptied, only Bryan, Scopes, and Malone were left. Bryan had not moved from his chair from the time that

64

Malone had started speaking. As Malone and his client went to leave, they passed by the older man. "Dudley," Bryan said, "that was the greatest speech I have ever heard." "Thank you, Mr. Bryan," Malone replied. "I am sorry it is I who had to make it."

On Friday, Judge Raulston decided that experts would not be allowed to testify. He agreed with the prosecution that the purpose of the trial was just to decide whether Scopes had broken the law. It seemed as if that might be the end for the defense team's case. But they were not willing to give up just yet.

The defense team's plan all along was to take the *Scopes* case to a higher court to challenge the constitutionality of the Butler Law. Now, they argued, it would only be fair if the evidence they hoped to present was made part of the court record. This way, the state Supreme Court justices could review it. To that end, the judge allowed the team to gather its expert testimony and then have it read into the record in open court.

When court adjourned for the weekend, most people assumed the trial was nearly over. The prosecution had rested its case earlier on Wednesday, and the defense did not seem to have any witnesses to call upon. As it turns out, the spectators and reporters who chose not to return to the courthouse on Monday ended up missing one of the greatest showdowns in legal history.

# The Great Showdown

When court was called into session on Monday morning, the defense team was allowed to read the expert testimony out loud so that it could be entered into the record. Once again, the jury was ordered outside.

After the lunch break, Judge Raulston ordered the entire trial to be moved outside. He had noticed a crack in the courtroom ceiling and was afraid it might collapse. Stands were set up outside, and before long more than 5,000 people had gathered under the hot sun to witness the end of the trial.

When defense attorney Arthur Garfield Hays stood up and called Bryan to testify, a ripple of shock flowed through the crowd—especially the prosecution team. All of the prosecuting

*Moving the trial outside gave everyone in town the opportunity to see two of the country's greatest speakers face off in court.*

attorneys, except for Bryan, began objecting. Once everyone quieted down, though, Bryan said that he had no problem testifying. He expected to have the same opportunity to question someone from the defense team as well. Once that was agreed to, William Jennings Bryan approached the witness stand, where he would be questioned by Darrow.

When Bryan took the stand, Clarence Darrow established Bryan's expertise in interpreting the Bible. The two men discussed how long Bryan had been studying Scripture, which was more than 50 years. Then Darrow came to the heart of the matter when he asked Bryan whether he believed everything in the Bible should be taken literally. "I believe everything in the Bible should be accepted as it is given there," Bryan replied.

Darrow continued to question Bryan about various stories from the Bible, often exposing the witness' lack of knowledge about anything outside of the religious arena:

> Darrow: *You believe the story of the flood to be a literal interpretation?*
> Bryan: *Yes, sir.*
> Darrow: *When was that flood?*

## THE JURY'S OUT

Once again, the jury was asked to leave the area while Bryan testified. The judge feared that some or all of Bryan's testimony would not be pertinent to the case and so would be inappropriate for them to hear. All in all, the jury heard less of the case than the spectators did. It has been estimated that the jury only spent a total of one hour in court during the eight-day trial.

Bryan: *I would not attempt to fix the date. The date is fixed, as suggested this morning.*
Darrow: *About 4004 B.C.?*
Bryan: *That has been the estimate of a man that is accepted today. I would not say it is accurate.*
Darrow: *That estimate is printed in the Bible?*
Bryan: *Everybody knows, at least, I think most of the people know, that was the estimate given.*
Darrow: *But what do you think that the Bible, itself says? Don't you know how it was arrived at?*
Bryan: *I never made a calculation.*
Darrow: *A calculation from what?*
Bryan: *I could not say.*
Darrow: *From the generations of man?*
Bryan: *I would not want to say that.*
Darrow: *What do you think?*
Bryan: *I do not think about things I don't think about.*
Darrow: *Do you think about things you do think about?*
Bryan: *Well, sometimes.*

Even Bryan's most dedicated supporters in the crowd had to laugh at how silly he sounded. Darrow then asked Bryan if he was aware of the civilizations that could trace their origins back further than 5,000 years. Mesopotamia, China, and Egypt all had well documented histories that proved they had lived before, during, and after the flood that Bryan claimed had wiped out the entire human race.

*Clarence Darrow's questioning of William Jennings Bryan (seated) is considered one of the greatest courtroom examinations in American history.*

Bryan responded that he was not satisfied with the evidence he had seen on that topic. But through continued questioning by Darrow, it became clear that Bryan knew little about archaeology, geology, or ancient civilizations. In fact, he did not even seem to understand what gravity was.

Finally Darrow asked Bryan whether he believed Earth had been created in six days. This, after all, was at the heart of the matter of the trial. Should the story of creation from the Bible be taken as truth, or should people accept the undeniable scientific evidence that supported the theory of evolution?

After lengthy questioning about whether each day mentioned in the Bible was made up of 24 hours or whether they were indistinct periods of time, Darrow got Bryan to make a huge blunder:

Bryan: *I think it would be just as easy for the kind of God we believe in to make Earth in six days as in six years or in 6,000,000 years or in 600,000,000 years. I do not think it important whether we believe one or the other.*
Darrow: *Do you think those were literal days?*
Bryan: *My impression is they were periods …*

By admitting that creation of Earth could have taken 6 million years as opposed to the six days stated in the Bible, Bryan had gone against the most important belief of his followers—that every word in the Bible had to be taken as fact. He had also proven the prosecution's point that the theory of evolution did not necessarily conflict with the Bible.

Prosecutor Stewart, realizing his associate's mistake, tried to come to his aid, asking, "What is the purpose of this examination?" But Bryan answered before the judge or even Darrow could.

Bryan said:

> *The purpose is to cast ridicule on everybody who believes in the Bible, and I am perfectly willing that the world shall know that these gentlemen have no other purpose than ridiculing every Christian who believes in the Bible.*

But Darrow quickly countered:

> *We have the purpose of preventing bigots and ignoramuses [ignorant people] from controlling the education of the United States and you know it—and that is all!*

Darrow continued questioning Bryan, whose answers became more and more absurd. Finally, hearing the laughter of the crowd that had once supported him, Bryan snapped:

> Bryan: *Your Honor, I think I can shorten this testimony. The only purpose Mr. Darrow has is to slur at the Bible, but I will answer his question. I will answer it all at once, and I have no objection in the world, I want the world to know that this man, who does not believe in a God, is trying to use a court in Tennessee—*
> Darrow: *I object to that.*
> Bryan, continuing: *—to slur at it, and while it will require time, I am willing to take it.*
> Darrow: *I object to your statement. I am exempting you on your fool ideas that no intelligent Christian on Earth believes.*

Seeing that the case was quickly turning into a shouting match, the judge ordered the questioning stopped. He excused Bryan from the witness stand and adjourned court for the day. In the space of an hour and a half, the tables had been turned, and Bryan's reputation lay in tatters.

The next morning, the judge decided to strike Bryan's testimony from the record. He did not feel it was relevant to the case. John Scopes was never called to the witness stand. Since it had already been established that he had broken the Butler Law by teaching evolution, there was no reason to have him testify at the trial. At that point, there was nothing left to do but call the jury in and instruct them on their duty.

Judge Raulston told them their only job was to decide whether Scopes had taught his students the theory of evolution. If so, the jury would have to find him guilty. Whether Scopes' lessons conflicted with the Bible was not an issue.

---

### DARROW'S RECOLLECTION OF THE DAY

Clarence Darrow later recalled what happened after his questioning of William Jennings Bryan:

When court adjourned it became evident that the audience had been thinking, and perhaps felt that they had heard something worthwhile. Much to my surprise, the great gathering began to surge toward me. They seemed to have changed sides in a single afternoon. A friendly crowd followed me toward my home. Mr. Bryan left the grounds practically alone. The people seemed to think he had failed and deserted his cause and his followers when he admitted that the first six days might have been periods of millions of ages long. Mr. Bryan had made himself ridiculous and had contradicted his own faith. I was truly sorry for Mr. Bryan.

Since it had been proven right from the start that Scopes had taught his students evolution, the judge was practically instructing the jury to come back with a guilty verdict. And after just nine minutes, that is exactly what it did. That was fine with the defense, though, since the team's real goal to take its case to a higher court.

*No one was surprised when the jury came back with a guilty verdict for John Scopes.*

After Scopes was found guilty and ordered to pay a $100 fine, he finally got a chance to have his say in court:

## A GENEROUS OFFER

It had been agreed from the beginning of the case that the ACLU would pay Scopes' fine if he were found guilty. William Jennings Bryan also offered to pay the $100 if the schoolteacher could not afford to pay it himself.

*Your Honor, I feel that I have been convicted of violating an unjust statute. I will continue in the future, as I have in the past, to oppose this law in any way I can. Any other action would be in violation of my ideal of academic freedom—that is, to teach the truth as guaranteed in our constitution, of personal and religious freedom. I think the fine is unjust.*

After several of the attorneys made closing statements, Raulston made one of his own. Though the judge did not mention Scopes by name, his words that day showed the respect he had for the young teacher's principles:

*It does not take any great courage for a man to stand for a principle that meets with the approval of public sentiment around him. But it sometimes takes courage to declare a truth or stand for a fact that is in contravention [opposed] to the public sentiment. ... [A] man who is big enough to search for the truth and find it, and declare it in the face of all opposition is a big man.*

At around noon on Tuesday, July 21, 1925, the so-called Great Monkey Trial was over. The crowds and most of the attorneys returned to their homes. Bryan stayed locally for a little while, visiting nearby towns to give speeches. That Sunday, after eating a big lunch, the 65-year-old went to his room to take a nap. He died in his sleep.

*Judge John Raulston was a religious man who did not believe in evolution. Still, he tried his best to remain fair throughout the trial.*

John Scopes never taught again. Some of the expert witnesses had set up a scholarship fund that enabled him to attend the University of Chicago, where he studied geology. He spent the rest of his life studying rocks.

In 1926, the ACLU brought the case to the Tennessee Supreme Court. The court did not overturn the county court's decision. But it did overturn Scopes' conviction because the judge—not the jury—had set Scopes' fine. According to Tennessee law, a judge was not allowed to set a fine for more than $50. Because Scopes' conviction had been overturned on this technicality, the ACLU could not bring its case to the next level, the U.S. Supreme Court. The Butler Law would stay on the books.

The fight over evolution in the classrooms was far from over, but it would take decades for a resolution to be reached.

# Slow Progress

By the 1940s, the fight between evolutionists and fundamentalists had faded. But there were still many Southern teachers who were afraid to teach evolution. Only a few textbooks in Tennessee mentioned Charles Darwin and evolution, and most high school teachers ignored the topic entirely. It was not until the 1960s that biology books and classes focused once again on evolution, a shift that was prompted more by the Soviet and American space race than anything else.

On October 4, 1957, the Soviet Union launched *Sputnik I*, the first artificial satellite to be successfully placed in orbit. *Sputnik*, which was about the size of a basketball and weighed 183 pounds (82.35 kilograms), orbited Earth in about

98 minutes. The successful mission marked the beginning of the space race between the United States and the Soviet Union. It also opened the door to a boom in advances in technology and science.

As a result of *Sputnik I*, the United States realized it was falling behind the rest of the world in

*The launch of Sputnik I started the space race between the Soviets and the Americans.*

education. Americans realized how important it was to focus on science in school and, in 1967, the Butler Law was finally repealed. Not long after, the anti-evolution laws in other states were also repealed.

The first such law to be declared unconstitutional by the U.S. Supreme Court was from Arkansas. In 1965, Susan Epperson, a biology teacher in Little Rock, brought a test case to court to challenge the constitutionality of anti-evolution laws.

Her case, *Epperson v. Arkansas*, reached the Supreme Court in 1968, where the law was declared unconstitutional. According to the court, it violated the First and 14th amendments to the Constitution. Just two years later, Mississippi's anti-evolution law was also declared unconstitutional—this time by the state Supreme Court. It was the last state law of its kind in the United States.

With the last of the anti-evolution laws abolished and evolution being taught in schools everywhere, many fundamentalists once again grew nervous. There was no way to keep evolution out of schools, and the teachings of the Bible could not be brought in. They had to develop a new plan.

## AND GOD CREATED MAN

In a Gallup Poll conducted in November 2004, 45 percent of peop questioned said they agreed with the statement, "God creat human beings pretty much in their present form at one time witl the last 10,000 years or so." And one-third of the respondents s they thought the Bible should be taken literally.

Throughout the 1970s, this group, now calling themselves creationists, argued that their theories deserved equal time in the classroom. They wanted educators to teach the Bible's story of creation along with the theory of evolution. They did not have success until 1981, when Act 590 was introduced in the Arkansas legislature.

The bill stated that teachers must cover "creation-science" along with "evolution-science" in any course where the origins of humankind were taught. On March 19, 1981, Governor Frank J. White signed the bill into law.

Again scientists, teachers, and other concerned citizens banded together to get the law overturned. In 1981, the ACLU supplied a team of attorneys to argue the constitutionality of the law. This time there were no famous attorneys; there was not even a jury. On January 5, 1982, the judge in the case ruled that creation-science was actually religion and not science. Because teaching religion in public schools is unconstitutional, he abolished the law.

A law called the Creationism Act had been passed in Louisiana in 1982. Five years later, that law was tested before the U.S. Supreme Court. On June 19, 1987, the court made the same ruling that had been made in the Arkansas case: creationism was religion. Teaching it in public schools violated the First Amendment, which guarantees the separation of church and state.

It looked as if creationists had been soundly defeated, but once again they found another way. In 1996, activists in Alabama succeeded in adding a disclaimer to biology textbooks. The disclaimer was a sticker, which read that evolution is a controversial theory that only some scientists accept. Of course, opponents to this argue that all reputable scientists accept evolution as fact. In 2005, when the issue was voted on again, the Alabama Board of Education voted to keep the disclaimer stickers in the state's textbooks.

Even at the beginning of the 21st century, the fight over what should be taught in schools continues. Anti-evolutionists are still lobbying for their theory, now called intelligent design, to be taught in schools. The idea behind intelligent design is that evolution could not have taken place—or continue to do so—without the guiding hand of a creator, in this case the Christian God. Like the creationists before them, their crusade is to have intelligent design taught alongside evolution in school.

In 2002, the Ohio Board of Education voted to change the science standards to encourage students to question the theory of evolution and to look for evidence for and against it. Though the new standards did not require the teaching of intelligent design, critics saw it as an opening for that theory to be brought into the classroom. In February 2006, however, the board, composed of new members, voted to get rid of the 2002 revised standards.

**A MESSAGE FROM THE ALABAMA STATE BOARD OF EDUCATION**

This textbook discusses evolution, a controversial theory some scientists present as a scientific explanation for the origin of Living things, such as plants, animals and humans.

No one was present when life first appeared on earth. Therefore, any statement about life's origins should be considered as theory, not fact.

The word "evolution" may refer to many types of change. Evolution describes changes that occur within a species. (White moths, for example, may "evolve" into grey moths.) This process is mircoevolution, which can be observed and described as fact. Evolution may also refer to the change of one living thing to another, such as reptiles into birds. This process, called marcoevolution, has never been observed and should be considered a theory. Evolution also refers to the unproven belief that random, undirected forced produced a world of living things.

There are many unanswered question about the origin of life which are not mentioned in your textbook, including:

- Why did the major groups of animals suddenly appear in the fossil record (know as the "Cambrain Explosion")?

- Why have no new major groups of living things appeared in the fossil record for a long time?

- Why do major groups of plants and animals have no transitional forms in the fossil record?

- How did you and all living things come to possess such a complete and complex set of "Instructions" for building a living body?

Study hard and keep an open mind. Someday, you may contribute to the theories of how living things appeared on earth.

*A disclaimer was added to science textbooks in Alabama in 1996.*

In the fall of 2005, the school board of Dover, Pennsylvania took an interesting approach to questioning evolution. It decided that the superintendent of schools would visit ninth-grade biology classes before the lesson on evolution and read from a statement, which said in part:

> *Because Darwin's theory is a theory, it is still being tested as new evidence is discovered. The theory is not a fact. Gaps in the theory exist for which there is no evidence. ... Intelligent design is an explanation of the origin of life that differs from Darwin's view. The reference book* Of Pandas and People *is available for students to see if they would like to explore this view. ... As is true with any theory, students are encouraged to keep an open mind.*

Concerned parents sued the school board, arguing that intelligent design was a religious idea, not a scientific one. In December 2005, a judge ruled in their favor, barring the statement from being read—and intelligent design from being taught—in the Dover public schools.

In 2005, the Kansas Board of Education voted to change the teaching standards for biology. The members wanted a statement included in textbooks that pointed out the "shortcomings" of the theory of evolution. When it was time to elect a new school board in 2006, though, the tables were turned. Advocates of intelligent design were voted out, and others regained control of the board. The disclaimer did not go into the books.

Scientists and educators agree that the intelligent design movement is not a scientific one, but a religious movement that is not based on scientific fact. Supporters of intelligent design have not done empirical studies to back their claims. They have, however, built a strong following. They have formed strong alliances with conservative Christians, and have gained the support of many influential politicians.

On the surface, the decades-long struggle over whether to teach evolution seems to be a conflict between science and religion. But what can get lost in this struggle is what many believe is really at stake: The guaranteed right of Americans to freedom of speech, freedom of religion, and the separation of church and state. As Clarence Darrow once said:

> *You can only be free if I am free. If even one person's freedom is limited, if just one person is deprived of his or her right to speak or to learn, then the liberty of all people is threatened.*

John Scopes and his team of attorneys began their fight to protect these basic freedoms more than 80 years ago. Over the years, others took up their cause. As the struggle to control what is taught in public schools continues, the citizens of the United States will be called upon again and again to stand up for and protect those freedoms.

# Timeline

**1543**

Nicolaus Copernicus publishes a book that proves Earth moves around the sun.

**June 1633**

Galileo is placed under house arrest for advocating the Copernican theory.

**December 27, 1831**

Charles Darwin signs on to the *H.M.S. Beagle* as an unpaid naturalist.

**1859**

Darwin's *The Origin of Species* is published.

**1910–1915**

The 12 religious pamphlets called *The Fundamentals* are published.

**1922**

A bill forbidding the teaching of evolution is introduced in Kentucky. It is defeated, but an anti-evolution resolution is passed.

**1923**

An anti-evolution bill is introduced—and defeated—in Florida.

**1924**

An anti-evolution bill is defeated in North Carolina. All biology books that cover evolution are removed from the public schools.

**March 13, 1925**

Tennessee's Butler Act is signed into law.

**May 4, 1925**

Tennessee newspapers print the ACLU's request for a test case volunteer.

**May 5, 1925**

During a meeting at Robinson's Drugstore, teacher John Scopes agrees to stand trial.

**May 25, 1925**

A special grand jury indicts John Scopes for violating the Butler Law.

**July 10, 1925**

*State of Tennessee v. John Thomas Scopes* officially begins with a re-indictment and jury selection.

**July 13, 1925**

The defense begins arguments to quash the indictment.

### July 15, 1925

The defense's motion to quash the indictment is denied by Judge John Raulston. Dr. Maynard Metcalf is introduced as a sample witness to help the judge decide whether to allow expert witnesses.

### July 17, 1925

Judge Raulston decides not to allow expert testimony in the case.

### July 20, 1925

Clarence Darrow questions William Jennings Bryan in one of the most celebrated courtroom examinations in history.

### July 21, 1925

The jury returns a guilty verdict. Raulston fines Scopes $100 for violating the Butler Law.

### January 15, 1927

The Tennessee Supreme Court overturns Scopes' conviction on a technicality, but the Butler Law stays on the books.

### May 16, 1967

The Tennessee Supreme Court overturns the Butler Law.

### October 18, 1968

The U.S. Supreme Court declares anti-evolution laws unconstitutional in *Epperson v. Arkansas.*

### 1970

Mississippi's anti-evolution law is declared unconstitutional by the state supreme court.

### March 19, 1981

Act 590, requiring the teaching of "creation-science" along with "evolution-science," is passed in Arkansas.

### January 5, 1982

Act 590 is declared unconstitutional.

### 1982

The Creationism Act is signed into law in Louisiana.

### June 19, 1987

The U.S. Supreme Court declares Louisiana's Creationism Act unconstitutional in *Edwards v. Aguillard.*

# Timeline

**1996**

Alabama adds a disclaimer to science textbooks stating that evolution is a controversial theory.

**2002**

The Ohio Board of Education changes its science teaching standards.

**2005**

The Dover, Pennsylvania, Board of Education drafts an "evolution theory" statement to be read in classrooms. The Kansas Board of Education votes to change science teaching standards.

**December 2005**

A judge rules against the Dover school board's statement.

**February 2006**

The Ohio Board of Education reverses its 2002 science teaching standards.

**August 2006**

School board elections result in a reversal of the Kansas Board of Education's science teaching standards.

## On the Web

For more information on this topic, use FactHound.

**1** Go to *www.facthound.com*

**2** Type in this book ID: 0756520185

**3** Click on the *Fetch It!* button. FactHound will find the best Web sites for you.

## Historic Sites

**The Scopes Museum-Rhea County Courthouse**
475 Market St.
Dayton, TN 37321

Designated a National Historic Landmark in 1977, the courthouse has been restored to the way it was in 1925 and includes a Scopes trial museum.

**Scopes Trial Annual Play and Festival**
Dayton Chamber of Commerce
107 Main St.
Dayton, TN 37321

A re-enactment of the trial is performed every July.

## Look For More Books in This Series

**Brown v. Board of Education:**
*The Case for Integration*

**The Chinese Revolution:**
*The Triumph of Communism*

**The Democratic Party:**
*America's Oldest Party*

**The Indian Removal Act:**
*Forced Relocation*

**The Japanese American Internment:**
*Civil Liberties Denied*

**The Progressive Party:**
*The Success of a Failed Party*

**The Republican Party:**
*The Story of the Grand Old Party*

A complete list of **Snapshots in History** titles is available on our Web site: *www.compasspointbooks.com*

# Glossary

**adjourn**
to close or end something

**allegory**
a fictional story with a message that is meant to teach a lesson

**bigotry**
treating someone of a different religious, racial, or ethnic group with hatred or intolerance

**censorship**
to limit what a person can say, write, or teach

**contradict**
to express an opposing point of view

**creationism**
the belief that the world and all its inhabitants were created exactly as it is written in the Bible's Book of Genesis

**crusade**
a battle or fight for which someone feels a great deal of emotion

**curricula**
courses taught in school

**defense**
the team that argues for the accused in a trial

**disclaimer**
a denial of an idea

**empirical**
based on experiment and observation

**evolution**
gradual changes occuring over time

**examination**
the questioning of a witness in a trial

**fundamentalist**
a Protestant who believes the Bible should be interpreted literally

**gloating**
delighting in one's own good luck or someone else's bad luck

**grand jury**
a group of people who meet to decide whether there is enough evidence to try someone for a crime

**intelligent design**
the belief that evolution could not have taken place, or continue to take place, without the guidance of a higher being

**organism**
a living plant or animal

**prosecution**
the team responsible for representing the state in a criminal trial

**Protestant**
a Christian denomination separate from the Roman Catholic Church or Orthodox Church

**relevant**
having to do with the matter at hand

**repealed**
officially canceled

**testimony**
evidence given by a witness in a trial

**theology**
the study of religious faith and practices

## Source Notes

### Chapter 1

Page 15, line 1: Frederick C. Foote, ed. *The Complete Scopes Trial Transcript: The Definitive Transcript of the Most Famous Court Trial in American History*, p. 243. eBookMall. 17 Oct. 2006. www.ebookmall.com/ebook/78295-ebook.htm

### Chapter 3

Page 31, line 9: *Tennessee Evolution Statutes. House Bill No. 185. Passed by the Sixty-Fourth General Assembly, 1925.* University of Missouri-Kansas City School of Law. 17 Oct. 2006. www.law.umkc.edu/faculty/projects/ftrials/scopes/tennstat.htm

Page 32, line 26: *The Complete Scopes Trial Transcript,* p. 170.

### Chapter 4

Page 40, line 13: John T. Scopes and James Presley. *Center of the Storm: Memoirs of John T. Scopes.* New York: Holt, Rinehart and Winston, 1967, p. 4.

Page 44, line 5: "Remembering the Scopes Monkey Trial." National Public Radio. 17 Oct. 2006. www.npr.org/templates/story/story.php?storyId=4723956

Page 46, line 14: Clarence Darrow. *The Story of My Life.* New York: Charles Scribner's Sons, 1932, pp. 244, 249.

Page 47, line 6: Ibid., p. 251.

### Chapter 5

Page 48, line 9: "Scopes Is Indicted in Tennessee for Teaching Evolution." *The New York Times,* 26 May 1925.

Page 51, line 4: "Fourth Day of Dayton Evolution Trial." 15 July 1925. 23 Oct. 2006. www.scopestrial.org/stday4.htm

Page 51, line 16: Ibid.

Page 52, line 4: *The Complete Scopes Trial Transcript,* p. 62.

Page 52, line 7: Ibid., p. 64.

Page 52, line 25: Ibid., p. 71.

Page 54, line 3: Ibid., p. 91.

Page 54, line 16: Ibid., p. 94.

## Source Notes

**Chapter 6**

Page 58, line 21: Ibid., p. 101.

Page 59, line 6: Ibid., p. 118.

Page 61, line 18: Ibid., p. 139.

Page 62, line 8: Don Nardo. *The Scopes Trial.* San Diego: Lucent Books, 1997, p. 62.

Page 62, line 13: *The Complete Scopes Trial Transcript,* pp. 141 and 150.

Page 65, lines 3 and 5: Mary Lee Settle. *The Scopes Trial: The State of Tennessee v. John Thomas Scopes.* New York: Franklin Watts, 1972, p. 94.

**Chapter 7**

Page 68, line 21: *The Complete Scopes Trial Transcript,* p. 227.

Page 68, line 27: "State v. Scopes: Trial Excerpts." University of Missouri-Kansas City School of Law. www.law.umkc.edu/faculty/projects/ftrials/scopes/day7.htm

Page 71, lines 11 and 27: *The Complete Scopes Trial Transcript,* p. 239.

Page 72, lines 2, 9, and 17: "State v. Scopes: Trial Excerpts."

Page 73, sidebar: *The Story of My Life,* p. 267.

Page 75, line 1: *The Complete Scopes Trial Transcript,* p. 250.

Page 75, line 14: Ibid., p. 254.

**Chapter 8**

Page 80, sidebar: Gallup Poll. 4 Nov. 2004. PollingReport.com. 2 Nov. 2006. www.pollingreport.com/science.htm

Page 84, line 1: "The Evolution Wars." *Time,* 15 Aug. 2005.

Page 85, sidebar: "Brown Professor on the Frontline of School Battle Over Evolution." *The Providence Journal,* 26 Nov. 2004.

Page 85, line 18: Arthur Blake. *The Scopes Trial: Defending the Right to Teach.* Brookfield, Conn.: The Millbrook Press, 1994, p. 60.

## SELECT BIBLIOGRAPHY

Darrow, Clarence. *The Story of My Life.* New York: Scribner's, 1932.

Foote, Frederick C., ed. *The Complete Scopes Trial Transcript: The Definitive Transcript of the Most Famous Court Trial in American History.* eBookMall.

Moran, Jeffrey P. *The Scopes Trial: A Brief History with Documents.* New York: Palgrave, 2002.

Olasky, Marvin N., and John Perry. *Monkey Business: The True Story of the Scopes Trial.* Nashville, Tenn.: Broadman and Holman, 2005.

Scopes, John T., and James Presley. *Center of the Storm: Memoirs of John T. Scopes.* New York: Holt, Rinehart and Winston, 1967.

Settle, Mary Lee. *The Scopes Trial: The State of Tennessee v. John Thomas Scopes.* New York: Franklin Watts, 1972.

## FURTHER READING

Blake, Arthur. *The Scopes Trial: Defending the Right to Teach.* Brookfield, Conn.: The Millbrook Press, 1994.

Hanson, Freya Ottem. *The Scopes Monkey Trial: A Headline Court Case.* Berkeley Heights, N.J.: Enslow Publishers, 2000.

Kraft, Betsy Harvey. *Sensational Trials of the 20th Century.* New York: Scholastic Press, 1998.

McGowen, Tom. *The Great Monkey Trial: Science vs. Fundamentalism in America.* New York: Franklin Watts, 1990.

Nardo, Don. *The Scopes Trial.* San Diego: Lucent Books, 1997.

# Index

1st Amendment, 36, 80, 81
14th Amendment, 80

**A**

academic freedom, 14, 42, 46, 47, 75
Act 590 (Arkansas), 81
agnosticism, 46
Alabama Board of Education, 82
American Civil Liberties Union (ACLU),
    36–37, 38, 40, 41, 47, 62, 75, 77, 81
American Railway Union, 45
anti-evolution legislation, 28, 30–31, 41, 42,
    44, 47, 49, 50, 80, 82
Arkansas, 80, 81

**B**

Bible, 10, 12, 14, 16, 17, 18, 27, 43, 48, 51,
    52, 54, 55, 56, 59, 64, 68, 69, 71, 72,
    80, 81
Bible Belt, 28, 30
Bill of Rights, 15, 36
Bryan, William Jennings, 13–14, 42–45, 46,
    47, 61–62, 63, 64–65, 66, 68–71, 71–72,
    73, 75, 76
Bryan, William Jennings, Jr., 47
Bush, George W., 85
Butler, John Washington, 31
Butler Law, 31–33, 34, 35, 36–37, 38, 39, 40,
    41, 49, 50, 51, 52, 55, 65, 73, 77, 80

**C**

censorship, 52
*Civic Biology* textbook, 39, 55
Congregational Church, 57
Constitution of the State of Tennessee, 49, 51
Constitution of the United States, 34–35,
    36, 42
constitutionality, 34–35, 36–37, 50, 65, 80,
    81
Copernicus, Nicolaus, 18
"creation-science," 81
creationism, 13, 14, 17, 18, 43, 48–49, 80,
    81, 82
Creationism Act (Louisiana), 81

**D**

Darrow, Clarence, 14–15, 45–46, 50, 52–53,
    55, 57, 58, 59–60, 62, 68–72, 73, 85
Darwin, Charles, 12, 19, 20–22, 23, 24, 39,
    62, 78, 84
Dayton High School, 10, 39
Dayton, Tennessee, 8, 10, 11, 12, 37, 38, 41,
    47, 50
Debs, Eugene V., 45
defense, 42, 45, 46, 47, 49, 50, 52, 53, 54, 55,
    56, 58, 59, 62–64, 65, 66, 68, 74
Democratic Party, 42, 46
Department of Labor, 42
disclaimer stickers, 82, 83, 84
Dover, Pennsylvania, 83–84

**E**

Empedocles (Greek scholar), 24
Epperson, Susan, 80
Epperson v. Arkansas, 80
evolution, 10, 12, 18, 19–20, 26–27, 28, 30,
    39, 40, 51, 56, 78, 80, 82
"evolution-science," 81

**F**

Ferguson, William, 39
finches, 20–21
fine, 31, 40, 74, 75, 77
First Amendment, 36, 80, 81
fossils, 18–19, 24, 25
Fourteenth Amendment, 80
freedom of religion, 51, 85
freedom of speech, 36, 47, 85
fundamentalists, 10, 12, 27, 28, 30, 31, 32,
    44, 46, 47, 61, 78, 80
The Fundamentals (religious pamphlets), 27

**G**

Galapagos Islands, 20, 22
Galileo, 18
genetic traits, 23
Godsey, John, 41, 42, 47
grand juries, 41, 48, 49

**H**

*H.M.S. Beagle*, 20, 21
Haggard, Wallace, 37, 41, 47
Hays, Arthur Garfield, 47, 49, 62, 66
Hicks, Herbert, 37, 41, 45, 47
Hicks, Sue, 37, 41, 45, 47

**I**

indictment, 41, 49, 50, 53
intelligent design, 82, 84–85

**J**

judge. See Raulston, John.
jury, 50, 57, 58, 59, 64, 66, 68, 73, 74, 77

**K**

Kansas Board of Education, 84
Kentucky, 28
Knoxville, Tennessee, 42

**L**

Lamarck, Chevalier de, 24

**M**

Malone, Dudley Field, 46–47, 49, 54–55,
    62–64, 65
McElwee, F. B., 47
McKenzie, Ben G., 47
McKenzie, J. Gordon, 47
"The Menace of Darwinism" speech
    (William Jennings Bryan), 44
Mendel, Gregor, 25
Metcalf, Maynard M., 57–58, 59
Milner, Lucille, 36
Mississippi, 80
Mississippi Supreme Court, 80
Monkey Trial, 10, 11
Morgan, Howard, 55

**N**

natural selection, 22–23
Neal, John R., 42, 47, 49, 51
Neanderthals, 24
North Carolina, 30

**O**

Ohio Board of Education, 82
*On the Origin of Species by Means of Natural
    Selection, or the Preservation of Favoured
    Races in the Struggle for Life* (Charles
    Darwin), 19, 21–22

**P**

Peay, Austin, 32–33
plea, 53
prosecution, 47, 54, 55, 56, 59, 62, 63, 64,
    65, 66, 71
Protestant religion, 10, 12, 27

**Q**

quashing an indictment, 49, 50, 53

**R**

radio broadcast, 8
Rappelyea, George, 37–38, 41
Raulston, John, 47, 48, 50, 53, 56–57, 65, 66,
    71, 73, 75, 76, 77
Rhea County Courthouse, 8, 12
Rhea County School Board, 37
Robinson, F. E. "Doc," 37, 40, 55
Robinson's Drugstore, 37, 38, 39, 55

**S**

scientific revolution, 16–17
Scopes, John, 10, 12, 13, 15, 39, 40–41, 47,
    48, 49, 54, 55, 56, 58, 64, 65, 73, 74–75,
    77, 85
Scopes, Thomas, 49
separation of church and state, 36, 81, 85
Shelton, Harry, 55
Soviet Union, 78, 79
space race, 78, 79
spectators, 58, 61, 62, 64, 65, 66, 68, 69, 72,
    75–76
*Sputnik I* satellite, 78–79
Stewart, A. Thomas, 47, 48, 54, 64, 71
Supreme Court (Mississippi), 80
Supreme Court (Tennessee), 37, 50, 65, 77
Supreme Court (United States), 35, 37, 77,
    80, 81
"survival of the fittest," 23

**T**

Tennessee, 8, 10, 31–32, 34, 37, 39, 47, 49,
    50, 72, 77, 78
Tennessee State Constitution, 49, 51
Tennessee Supreme Court, 37, 50, 65, 77
theories, 58
traits, 23

**U**

U.S. Constitution, 34–35, 36
U.S. Supreme Court, 35, 37, 77, 80, 81

**V**

verdict, 37, 74

**W**

White, Frank J., 81
White, Walter, 37, 55
Wilson, Woodrow, 42, 43
witnesses, 50, 55, 56–60, 65, 68–73, 77
World War I, 43

## ABOUT THE AUTHOR

Stephanie Fitzgerald has been writing nonfiction for children for more than 10 years. Her specialties include history, wildlife, and popular culture. Stephanie lives in Stamford, Connecticut, with her husband, Brian, and daughter, Molly.

## IMAGE CREDITS